GRAND CANYON
A VISUAL STUDY

TITLE PAGE PHOTO: SUNSET, SOUTH RIM

ISBN O-939365-15-4 (Paper)
       O-939365-20-0 (Cloth)

Printed in Singapore
First Edition 1991
Second Edition 1993 (Revised)
Third Edition 1997

ACKNOWLEDGEMENTS

We wish to thank Ellis Richard, Chief Park Naturalist, his
dedicated staff and the National Park Service and its employ-
ees, both past and present. It is due to their foresight and hard
work that wonderlands such as Grand Canyon are still here
for each of us to enjoy. It is up to each of us, as individuals,
to make certain our own use is consistent with the long-term
needs of these natural temples.

DEDICATION

This book is dedicated
to those who stop;
to see, to hear, to smell, to taste, to feel,
not just to know,
but to understand.

SIERRA PRESS, INC.

P.O. BOX 430, EL PORTAL, CA. 95318

CONTENTS

INTRODUCTION

"The most beautiful and most pro-found emotion we can experience is the sensation of the mystical. It is the source of all science."

Albert Einstein

It may be, as Lt. Joseph C. Ives stated in 1857, that this is a "prof-itless locality" in an "altogether valueless" region, or it may be that this is "the most sublime spec-tacle on earth" as John Wesley Powell proclaimed in 1872. That the same locality should elicit such contradictory comments is not sur-prising; each man brought his own priorities, his own expectations.

What should today's visitor ex-pect upon first arriving at the Grand Canyon? Expect contradiction! Powell described it as "awful, sub-lime and glorious". Pretty contra-dictory stuff.

It is a place of myth and a place of mathematics.

It is a vertical landscape com-posed of horizontal elements.

It is forests of spruce, aspen and fir and deserts of sand, yucca and prickly pear.

It is ravens soaring wing tip to wing tip with their own shadows — hundreds of feet <u>below</u> you.

It is as young as this year's wild-flowers and older than life on earth.

It is a land of deafening silence and the thunder of rapids on the Colorado River.

It is a million acres of sun-scorched sandstone and luxurious spring-fed hanging gardens.

It is cottonwood leaves rustling in the breeze; it is rattlesnakes buzzing among the rocks.

It appears timeless and unchanging, yet it is clear evidence of the changing nature of our planet. This landscape of sandstone, siltstone, mudstone, limestone, shale, granite, schist and gneiss was left here by ancient oceans, swamps, lagoons, rivers and deserts.

The Colorado is a river that has been described as "too thick to drink and too thin to plow."

It is the blinding glare of a midsummer noon and the warming embrace of a winter sunset.

It is the temples of Zoroaster, Buddha, Cheops and Ra and it is Vasey's Paradise, Elve's Chasm and Deer Creek.

It is the opalescent turquoise of Havasu Creek and the foaming red rage of liquid mud flash flooding down canyons.

It is scorpions, rattlesnakes and spiders and it is deer, elk, bighorn and squirrels.

It is "too vast, too complex, too grand for verbal description."

What should the first-time visitor expect? Expect the unexpected! Hope for one small glimpse of insight, one moment of breathless, speechless awe. Hope for a vision of understanding, of wisdom. Hope for "the sensation of the mystical."

South Rim

*There is nothing that communicates the absolute
astonishment of viewing this giant crevasse.
i cannot completely prepare, for my mind has
always had a gauge to measure things by.
But how do i calibrate this infinite void?*

*Edge of nothingness
Expansive space
Immeasurably wide
Unfathomably deep
Utterly quiet
Hauntingly peaceful*

Everyone whispers and no one knows why.

The Earth speaks...And it has my undivided attention.

SUNSET, HOPI POINT

SINKING SHIP VIEWPOINT, WINTER

SUNRISE, MATHER POINT

VIEW FROM HERMIT CREEK TRAIL

CORPUSCULAR RAYS AT SUNSET

STORM SEEN FROM MATHER POINT

MOHAVE WALL, SUNSET

WINTER SUNSET FROM HOPI POINT

VIEW FROM CAPE SOLITUDE

LIGHTNING NEAR O'NEILL BUTTE

SUNSET FROM MORAN POINT

CANYON DETAIL FROM MORAN POINT

RAINBOW OVER LITTLE COLORADO RIVER GORGE 24

SUNRISE FROM YAKI POINT

JUNIPERS NEAR DESERT VIEW

Below the Rim

ZOROASTER TEMPLE

Cool rock--hot sun.
Lost without the ticking i gauge my life by.
Captured in
  Rock time
  Seed time
  Water time
  Dying time
my
  Life time

Dizzy from the radiating quality of rock and light.

i stand before

  The City of Gods
  The Valley of Kings
  Sipapuni

Phenomenal layers of colored rock.
Canyons within The Canyon.
Thousands of feet between here and anywhere.

Time stands still.
Hours flash in moments.
Shadows grow to meet the rising moon.
Moonbeams dance across the land.
Stars chandelier the black of midnight.

The Earth speaks...And i hear it.

MULES AND RIDERS, BRIGHT ANGEL TRAIL

HILLTOP RUIN, LOOKING NORTH

TAPEATS SANDSTONE, DEER CREEK GORGE 32

PRICKLY PEAR CACTUS

BUDDHA TEMPLE FROM PLATEAU POINT

WHIPPLE'S YUCCA ON THE ESPLANADE

ANGULAR LIMESTONE, SADDLE CANYON

UTAH AGAVE, PHANTOM CREEK

TRAVERTINE BELOW HAVASU FALLS

MONKEYFLOWER, KANAB CREEK

MOONRISE NEAR HOUSEROCK RAPID

48

the River

COLORADO RIVER FROM NANKOWEAP CREEK

Silted water wheels and splashes,
Over boulder-strewn riverbed.
Sandy beaches at my feet,
Blue skies overhead.

Sprays catch the sun and prism.
A mucky rainbow (to my delight),
Arches a tiny bird within,
Obscure and out of sight.

The bird walks the river bottom
Doing brave and daring feats.
But it really is no problem,
Since this is how he eats.

Sunset brings a roof of flame.
i walk beneath its fire.
Running water reflects the same,
i stand with great desire.

Sandals off, slipped in the ooze,
And squished between my toes a mire.
Complete am i with Mother Earth,
Her wind, water and fire.

Come, quiet evening
And twinkles of the night.
Ravens rest and crickets sing,
Bats swoop in flight.

Nocturnal beings--great and small,
Begin to take a peak.
Ventures out a ringtail cat,
The language bullfrogs speak.

Dawn hues, morning breeze,
Clouds paint pastel.
Shadows first see light,
A heavy tropic smell.

Dreams gone by, midnight songs,
Deep sleep, i am well.
Excited for this brand-new day,
And secrets it will tell.

The Earth speaks...And i listen.

MARBLE CANYON BELOW BADGER CREEK

ROCK AND REFLECTIONS, NORTH CANYON

DANA BUTTE, EVENING LIGHT

VISHNU SCHIST NEAR MONUMENT CREEK

LITTLE COLORADO RIVER CANYON

BOULDERS NEAR BUCK FARM CANYON

PRICKLY PEAR, LITTLE COLORADO RIVER GORGE

REFLECTIONS OF PALISADES OF THE DESERT IN TANNER RAPID

COLORADO RIVER, MARBLE CANYON

POLISHED LIMESTONE BOULDER

MARBLE CANYON AT THE MOUTH OF NORTH CANYON

North Rim

Wild turkeys run amuck.
Bobcats print the land.
Waist-high grass shines in sun
Where hungry elks will stand.

Squirrels frolic through the trees,
Swinging limb to limb.
Stop to nibble on a cone,
And find its seeds within.

The air is thin and cooler here,
Morning sun warms behind.
First light strikes in front of me,
That glowing golden kind.

i look within the canyon,
Temples illuminate
i reflect upon these last few days,
And i appreciate.

The Earth speaks...And i finally understand!

REDWALL LIMESTONE, CAPE ROYAL

VIEW FROM POINT SUBLIME

ASPEN LEAVES, AUTUMN

BARE ASPENS, LATE AUTUMN

LIMESTONE LEDGE, BRIGHT ANGEL POINT

WEST WALL OF WOTAN'S THRONE, SUNSET

GRANITE NARROWS, DEER CREEK TRAIL

ASPENS NEAR POINT IMPERIAL

VISHNU TEMPLE, SUNSET

GRASSES ABOVE TEMPLE BUTTE

MT. HAYDEN FROM POINT IMPERIAL

SUNRISE INSPIRATION, TOROWEAP POINT

i query the tongues of this land.
For i must
    Recognize the foreverness of blue sky.
    Learn the million languages of life.
    Understand the past to gain the present.
Hear the
    Voices in muted stone.
    Silent songs of Earth.
    Trees talk.
    Laughing waters.
    Whispers of wind.
    Birth of grass.

This place is a living history book.
The teacher of before.
Instructs me in the anatomy of
    Today.
    Now.
    Here.

Oh to be learned,
    Unlocking secret things.
    Gaining Earths' knowledge,
    In virtually everything.

Oh to be fulfilled,
    Enjoying Nature's beauty.
    Taking peace and solace
    In everything i see.

Oh to be simple,
    Curiously walking land.
    Sorting life's complexities,
    By simply sifting sand.

Oh to be prudent,
    In doing what i can.
    Rightly divining the word of truth,
    As it applies to man.

The Earth speaks...And it has my undivided attention...Always.

GRAND CANYON NOTES
by Jim Wilson

COLORADO PLATEAU

In order to understand the Grand Canyon's origin one must first realize that this great feature is but a small, albeit important, piece of a much larger puzzle. The Canyon reflects the unleashed carrying and erosive power of the Colorado River and its tributaries. Located in the southwestern corner of a geological province scientists call the Colorado Plateau, this 130,000-square-mile geologic province teems with scenic treasures. Here water is both creator and sustainer of life. Although man-made highways cut through this region, allowing us easy access to Nature's handiwork, the network of watercourses that tentacle the province represent the true method of transportation. This network is dominated by the Colorado River and its tributaries. On this high desert plateau water arrives infrequently. However, it is usually in quantities sufficient to spark flash flooding. This raw, unharnessed power is responsible, in large part, for carving the chasms seen throughout this region. In addition to water, the forces of cataclysmic uplift, grit-bearing winds, freeze-expansion-thaw and gravity have played contributing roles in sculpting the colorful ridges, mesas, buttes, pinnacles, bridges and arches of this land. Nearly two billion years of Earth's history can be observed in its canyons. Stories of ancient oceans, lakes, lagoons and deserts are revealed in multi-hued sedimentary layers. Ages of vulcanism are described in igneous rocks and unanswered questions can be found in metamorphic ones. Elevation plays a major role here, ranging from over 12,000 feet in the La Sals and San Francisco Peaks to little more than 1,200 feet at the point where the Colorado River emerges from the Grand Canyon at Lake Mead. The biotic communities which exist on the Colorado Plateau are as diverse as these elevations would suggest.

VIEW FROM SOUTH RIM

When viewing this canyon, cut from western to eastern horizon, it seems obvious to the first-time visitor that erosion must have been the primary tool of creation for this deep chasm. This explanation works well to explain recent history, that of the past six million years. However, while marveling at its depth, one cannot help but notice the horizontal layering of various colored and textured rocks. A total of twenty-one sedimentary and metamorphic rock formations have been identified, stacked one atop another revealing nearly two billion years of nature's handiwork. Scientists tell us the earth is 4.6 billion years old; here we can study more than one-third of this time period. From South Rim the most obvious layers are those including, and above, the Tonto Plateau, that broad platform which stretches from the wall to the edge of the Inner Canyon. This upper 4,000 feet of the canyon was deposited during the Paleozoic era, from 250 to 550 million years ago. These layers tell the story of the advance and retreat of no less than seven oceans, a Sahara-like desert and several lagoons. Below the Paleozoic strata are older, Pre-Cambrian rocks. These eight sedimentary strata, called the Grand Canyon Supergroup, include, among others, Shinumo Quartzite and Bass Limestone formations. Their ages are approximately one billion years. At some point after their creation, but before the overlying strata were laid down, the Grand Canyon Supergroup was broken into several tilted, north-to-south mountain ranges. Through the fault-blocking process portions of the Supergroup were uplifted while others dropped. Subsequent erosion removed all but the lowest of these blocks. This explains why we can observe only isolated pockets of this Supergroup throughout the length of Grand Canyon. The harder metamorphic and igneous rocks of the Inner Canyon

were born of intense heat while the sedimentary history of the upper layers reflects a diverse series of quiet oceans, shallow seas, swamps, lagoons and wind-blown deserts. After one's astonishment and sense of wonder settles in, one becomes aware that there is more to Grand Canyon National Park than a chasm. Life along the rim is rich and abundant. Ravens soar the thermals and squirrels scamper along the rim. The most basic forms of life one may observe are lichens and mosses, both are well adapted to this semi-arid environment. Common shrubs include cliffrose, fernbush and mountain mahogany. Forests of the South Rim are predominantly ponderosa pine, pinyon pine and Utah juniper. In addition, blooming throughout the summer season is a diverse variety of colorful wildflowers. The rim and surrounding forests are rich in wildlife, including mule deer, tassel-eared squirrels, black bear, wild turkey and various rodents, as well as many species of birds.

BELOW THE RIM

Visitors descending below the South Rim encounter, one by one, the diverse layers of sediment laid down millions of years ago. First limestone, then sandstone, then shale.

The question inevitably arises as to the differences between each layer. Science tells us that limestone results from the deposition of calcium carbonate, either from sea water or from dying prehistoric life forms such as trilobites, molluscs or brachiopods. These two sources, sometimes acting alone and sometimes together, combined with time and intense pressure, result in the formation of limestone. Sandstone is composed of grains of sand while shale is made up of silt and clay. Time, natural "cement" and pressure mold each into unique layers of stone. Each has its own characteristics and reacts differently to erosion. Limestone and sandstone tend to form cliffs and ledges while shale, being weaker, tends to form slopes. While descending alongside these multi-hued layers of sedimentary stone we are reminded that each layer was deposited many millions of years ago. "Millions of years ago" is a phrase that leaves most visitors glassy-eyed. For example, how can someone who is only able to trace his own ancestry but five generations fathom "millions of years ago". Let's take the Redwall Limestone formation. It is easy to understand that it is 400 to 650 feet thick, but as one saunters, by trail, "through" the Redwall keep in mind that it took 1 million to 1.6 million years to lay down this single formation. Also keep in mind

that this layer was deposited approximately 330 million years ago. How long in human terms is that? Today a human generation averages 25 years. One million years would see 40,000 human generations come and go. Standing in admiration of the great Redwall it is mind-boggling to think that 13.2 million human generations would have passed since its formation! As one continues to descend the trail alongside each sedimentary layer it becomes obvious that an incomprehensible amount of time has passed since they were deposited.

THE COLORADO RIVER

The first Europeans, members of Coronado's expedition, gazed into the Grand Canyon from near today's East Rim Drive. One of them estimated the river far below to be a mere six feet wide. Upon their return from a long, exhaustive and unsuccessful attempt at crossing the chasm several conquistadores told of a great wide river and rocks taller than the Tower of Seville. Modern "explorers", upon hiking the canyon or floating the river, experience this same awe-inspiring feeling. The river flowing deep in the canyon is the same one responsible for carving this chasm. As one peers into Grand Canyon from Yavapai Point it measures nearly ten miles from rim to rim and one mile deep. How wide is ten miles? The world-famous Golden Gate Bridge is 1.5 miles long. If it were possible to connect the North Rim and the South Rims with a man-made span it would take seven Golden Gate Bridges constructed end to end. How deep is one mile? Horizontally, one mile of paved highway seems trivial, at 60 miles per hour a modern automobile will travel that one mile in one minute. But one vertical mile surpasses five Empire State Buildings placed one atop another. Interview any fatigued hiker as he emerges from a round trip hike to the Colorado River, he will surely have volumes to speak regarding that single vertical mile! Whether viewing or exploring the Grand Canyon, the question is asked "Where has the excavated earth gone?" The answer is it was, and continues to be, carried away by the Colorado River and its tributaries. The power of this river is illustrated by the fact that the excavation from the end of Marble Canyon to Grand Wash Cliffs was accomplished in just the last six million years. By geologic standards that is a relatively short period of time. It is difficult to comprehend how all the missing earth could have been moved by what appears to be a relatively insignificant body of water. However, a stream or river's ability to carry material away increases exponentially during flood stage. It has been calculated that, prior to 1963, the average load moved by the Colorado was nearly 400,000 tons of earth per day. This means that if the load were placed in a series of five-ton dump trucks, it would require 80,000 trucks each 24-hour day to accomplish the same work carried out by the river. Still too great to imagine? Then consider that as you walk the Kaibab Suspension Bridge, on the way to Phantom Ranch, at the average rate of two miles per hour, nearly 139 of those dump trucks would have passed beneath your feet. With the completion of the Glen Canyon Dam in 1963, the wild and unpredictable river was harnessed and, consequently, its ability to move earth was greatly reduced. Today the average load is approximately 80,000 tons per day or only about one-fifth of its previous tonnage. The rock and sand extracted from Grand Canyon now lies downstream, behind Hoover Dam and on the floor of the Imperial Valley, creating the massive delta where the river empties into the Gulf of California. The complete story of the creation of the Grand Canyon is still not fully understood, but suffice it to say that the complex process continues, even as each visitor stands and gazes across to a distant rim.

The North Rim of Grand Canyon National Park is almost always described in comparison to South Rim: 'it is higher than...', 'it is less visited than...' or 'it is more isolated than...', etc. While those comparisons are correct, above all, North Rim is stunningly beautiful on its own merits. When visiting North Rim, keep in mind that common forces created each rim, yet each rim possesses unique qualities. Exploring North Rim requires persistence. Some viewpoints along the Kaibab Plateau are accessible by paved road but all others, from Grand Wash Cliffs on the west to Grand Canyon Lodge on the east, require traveling many miles by foot or primitive road in order to reach the desired viewpoint. North Rim is made up of four distinct plateaus, each a world unto itself. Rising from Grand Wash Cliffs is the Shivwits Plateau, a pinyon-juniper woodland interspersed with sage, yucca, cacti and some ponderosa pine. At approximately 5,000 feet in elevation, it is classified as a high desert. Separating Shivwits Plateau and its neighbor, Uinkaret Plateau, are the Hurricane Cliffs. Uinkaret is a wedge-shaped plateau which narrows as it approaches the canyon rim. Its environment is much like that of the Great Basin, containing vast stretches of sage, blackbrush and shadscale. Its most prominent fea-

tures are the remnants of "recent" volcanic activity. Approximately one million years ago this area was an active volcanic zone, oozing molten lava from fissures opened by movement along fault zones. To the east, Uinkaret is bounded by the Toroweap Fault and the Kanab Plateau, a flat, treeless plain most noted for the stunning water-cut chasm Kanab Creek has carved. The canyon slices through millenniums of sedimentary layers before joining the Colorado River. This plateau is home to large populations of deer, coyote and black-tailed jackrabbits. At the eastern edge of the Kanab Plateau rises the uplifted Kaibab Plateau. This is the most visited area of North Rim. Lying between 7,000 and 9,000 feet above sea level it is the only area within the park where visitors can experience a lush sub-alpine spruce-fir forest. Kaibab Plateau is subjected to deep, cold winters, averaging 120 inches of annual snowfall, and cool summers. It is also home to a varied flora and fauna. Found here is the Kaibab squirrel, indigenous to the Kaibab Plateau. One can also observe mule deer, elk, bobcats and, if fortunate, mountain lions. Bird species include Williamson's sapsucker, western bluebird, black-tailed grosbeak, western meadowlark and, of course, the ever-present raven. High elevation and wet winters helped create, and still perpetuate, a series of montane meadows which support many species of grasses and colorful wildflowers. North Rim offers visitors unimaginable beauty as well as an ample supply of peace and solitude. It needs no comparison to any other area of the park or, for that matter, the Colorado Plateau.

The Grand Canyon is an incredible spectacle, a classic example of erosion unequalled anywhere on earth. It is the grand climax of the Colorado Plateau, the sum total of all the power nature has released into this geologic province. Grand Canyon is a park made up of many ecological worlds, including the subalpine forests of North Rim, the ponderosa pine forests of South Rim, the high desert-like Tonto Plateau and a Sonoran Desert environment at river level. In addition, there are untold micro-climes interspersed throughout, each possessing unique characteristics. One can be overwhelmed by a first visit to Grand Canyon and feel comfortable after several visits, but few, if any, have ever gained a complete mastery of all that this park en-

compasses. Its allure and complexities demand that one return again and again in order to satisfy the thirst for understanding.

PHOTOGRAPHIC CREDITS

Mary Allen: 62.
Chris Crossland: 12,35.
Eduardo Fuss: 22,30.
Gary Ladd: 14,19,20,32,36,38,41,42,43,44,46,47
  48,50,56,59,61,63,64,65,69,74,78,83,84,85,86.
George Lamont: 28.
Mark and Jennifer Miller: Cover.
Jeff Nicholas:1, 4, 5, 11,15,18,27,49,54,87,90,91,93,94 95.
Pat O'Hara: 39,45,67,76,77,79,80.
Arlene Pier: 66.
Greg Probst: 13,24,26,81.
Randall K. Roberts: 88.
John Telford: 8,72.
Tom Till: 6,21,23,31,55,60.
Larry Ulrich: 16,34,52,53,57,58,68,70,71,75,82.
Jim Wilson: 9,10,17,25,33,37,40,92.
Copyrights to all photographs remain with the artist.

CREDITS

Poetic Text by Lynn Wilson
Introduction by Jeff Nicholas
Canyon Notes by Jim Wilson
Edited by Ardeth Huntington
Design by Jeff Nicholas
Back Cover Illustration by Jeff Nicholas

Layout and graphic design performed on a Macintosh® SE
utilizing Aldus PageMaker® and Microsoft Word®. All texts
set in Palatino and Optima Typefaces by MacinType, Fresno,
Ca. Color separations and printing coordinated by Tien Wah
Press, Ltd., Berkeley, Ca.